Agapé: Heaven & Earth

Agapé
Heaven & Earth

Bob MacKenzie

edited by Faye Batchelor & Nancy Wills

Dark Matter
a Canadian publisher
Kingston, Canada

© 2015 by Dark Matter Press and The Author

All rights reserved. No part of this publication may be reproduced, stored in a retrieval system, or transported in any form or by any means, electronic, mechanical, photocopying, recording, or otherwise without prior written permission of the publisher.

Library and Archives Canada Cataloguing in Publication

MacKenzie, Bob, 1947-
[Poems. Selections]
Agapé : heaven & earth / Bob MacKenzie ; edited by
Faye Batchelor & Nancy Wills.

Poems.
Includes index.
ISBN 978-0-9916858-6-8 (pbk.)

I. Batchelor, Faye, editor II. Wills, Nancy, editor
III. Title. IV. Title: Heaven and earth.

PS8575.K424A6 2015   C811'.54   C2015-900936-7

I see my light come shining
From the west unto the east
                    Bob Dylan

Foreword

Several years ago, my then editor Faye Batchelor and I worked together on the entire body of my work as a poet. From this collection, Faye and I organized the poems into several volumes on different themes. Faye's excellent collaboration in this process led to a varied and interesting selection of manuscripts. Preparation for this work with Faye required that I revisit all of my poems written over a span of almost five decades, read them, and categorize them.

This was a fascinating experience, like going through all the old photo albums after the kids have grown up and left home. There was some nostalgia certainly, but I also found I'd achieved enough distance to see my poems objectively and learn about my progress and growth as a poet. I discovered themes and resonances that I had never noticed before. I also developed a far clearer idea of what it is that I write about. I'm sure this journey into my past has had a positive effect on my recent poetry.

After we had sent a couple of the manuscripts to publishers, Faye and I determined that this was not the way we wanted to go. Our intention was to take a step back and look at the poems from a different perspective before getting them published...but then other priorities overtook both Faye and me.

In 2013 and again this year, I came back to this project with renewed vigour and focus. I teamed up with a new editor, Nancy Wills, and we set out to create one longer manuscript that would be a retrospective of my half-century writing poetry. This was quite a process. First, Nancy and I independently went through hundreds of poems, grouping them into themes and subjects. Once we had both done that, we met and collated our respective lists into a form we felt was workable. In the end, we saw that an over-arching theme of love flowed through the collection. To bring further order, we grouped our several sub-themes under the two main themes, one relating to romantic love and spirituality and one to more worldly forms of love such as we have for family, nature, and the earth, among others.

Although these poems span almost fifty years, there is no chronological order to this book. Instead the poems are aggregated by theme and by synchronicity with adjacent poems. This was an aesthetic decision we had made to present the poems in a natural progression rather than by the dates on which they were written. Once we had read the completed manuscript, Nancy and I were pleased with the result. What was at first a pot-pourri of styles and content had become a wonderfully cohesive volume. I hope that you, as reader of these poems, will agree.

Bob MacKenzie

Table of Contents

Heaven

"Cry morning poet"	1
"sun shine on my world"	2
"never my forté"	3
"This pad is thin, so turn the page"	4
"Flowers like beanstalks jack up the blue"	5
"Leaf buds opening"	6
"He came packed in straw,"	7
"Gethsemane night,"	8
"Birthday celebrants"	9
"Ask, 'Was Adam a mushroom?'"	10
Although Adam	11
12:00 Midnight–TBA	12
Across the Water	13
autumn scene / across / the water	14
Rendezvous	15
After the Magician: Before the Musicians	16
"Who are you?"	18
These Eyes	21
after the flood	23
"Like Omar's guests,"	24
Life in a Bottle	25
Flying	26
"Some times of night the world seems far away"	27
"Do we each stand on our own shrinking line"	28
"On walking through the stacks of books..."	29
Last Call	30
"A world in the mirror"	31
"you are"	32
"the grey people linger in the periphery"	33
Twenty Four	34
"Time"	35
Focus Time	36
Passing Time	37
our small eternity	38

Table of Contents

"The lamp in the ceiling will burn out soon"	39
Bolex	40
Snapshot, December 17, 2013	43
Conspiracy	44
Hell is a coalmine	45
Life Underground	46
"When the sea has passed me by"	48
How Do I Remember	49
Time and the Prophet	51
Bee	52
Tree	53
The Cutter	54
One Last Move	55
Phase Shift	56
Behind	57
Silent Shadows	58
Other Winds	59
"Beware cold wind, the heat of day"	60
The Girl	61
"A flower opened this morning—"	66
Trip	67
"I live"	68
Communion	69
Hymn	70
Playing Tag	71
Soaring	72
Lesson 68	73
Flight Training	74
Fly	75
Earth that is Me breathes every Moon	76
Positive Café	77
"A strange word"	78
Love	79

Table of Contents

Earth

"First robin of spring"	80
"against white snow fields"	81
"Your mind and mine meet"	82
"baseball metaphors crack"	83
Child Paints	84
"Winter's artist's hand"	85
Summer Somewhere	86
"I remember the roses growing wild"	87
"Autumnlike before our springdance"	88
Light	89
"Christina, mind child living"	90
Two Girls	91
Oak	92
A Romance I: Guinevere	93
A Romance II: The Quest	94
A Romance III: The Grail	95
A Romance IV: Changes	96
A Romance V: Careering	97
A Romance VI: Affirmation	98
A Romance VII: Till Death Doe	99
Masts	100
Girl on a Swing	101
Randolph	102
trapeze	103
Flirtation	104
meeting	105
"Love song"	106
"If she is a goddess"	107
"My love for you shall remain quiet and soft..."	108
I Would Photograph You	109
"Hidden in back alleys they kiss; the lovers"	110
"If a thousand thousand poets' clever"	111

Table of Contents

Red String	112
soft my angel sleeps	113
Flight Risk	114
The Uncaged Bird	115
"mostly I'm missing you"	116
you live here	117
"Even when you are not here with me"	118
Beyond Convergence: The Whistle Dying	119
"outside the office"	120
Edge	121
grey is also a colour	128
"Restaurant people,"	129
Sidewalk	130
Studio	131
"I stand in the room where the painter was."	132
Mason Jar	133
Transferred	134
portrait	135
"In the prairies and mountains of the west"	136
The Train	137
"City life,"	138
"Looking through windows:"	139
"dark clouds embracing"	140
"Thunder and lightning,"	141
Cloudburst	142
Alberta	143
Inside Me	144
"don't be mad at me"	145
"The words are not the same,"	151
The New Police	152
Rainbow	153
Marathon	154
Circle the Wagons	155
America	159
scene	162

Table of Contents

"Do you laugh"	164
Elsa	165
"Furnace burning hot"	166
"The missing people mingle"	167
"Winter"	168
"White is forever"	169
"One by one the quiltsquares spiral"	170
"Red Sky and Rockies"	171
"Scrubland bison graze,"	172
Again turn the jar,"	173
Indian Summer	174
Dawn a Rose	175
"The news of the world"	176

Heaven

Cry morning poet
Night has fallen from the trees—
Wind sings your song now.

sun shine on my world
wash each garden with colour
paint the black sky blue

never my forté
these brief delicate flowers:
Japanese poems

This pad is thin, so turn the page
So slowly I can read each line
Of words of wisdom for my age;
A page, a year, of brown, of white.

Each year we tear the sheet of white
To free the brown beneath for use
To fill with ink both dark and bright—
Again, we turn the other leaf.

Flowers like beanstalks jack up the blue
Colourful paintpots lining their tops
Silver round globelets falling to you
Raindrops silver flowertop treasures.

Day again breaks with colours splashing
Shower bathing first thing in the day
Thunder rumble gnashing giant teeth;
Who would not give beans for such a day?

Leaf buds opening,
Forty days and nights of rain–
Who pilots the boat?

He came packed in straw,
"This side up", but durable–
His name is now gilt.

Gethsemane night,
Broken olive branch   a seed—
Morning is coming.

Birthday celebrants
Merrily repay the tree
On winter hillsides.

Ask, "Was Adam a mushroom?"
Say, "Look at his spore–
What other weed could there be?"

Although Adam

Though the Serpent seduced her with an apple and his eyes
And though Eve was meant to come back to Adam in the end
Though there was nothing Adam could do about it but wait
And though it was he she said she loved more than any other
She told Adam she must meet the Serpent in the garden

Adam waited alone in the garden for Eve to come
Unaware of anything but his raw nerves flayed naked
As his aching heart beat angry rhythm against his ribs
Although even now he knew there was nothing he could do
She'd told Adam she must meet the Serpent in the garden

In the beginning the Serpent seemed innocent enough
Although even then there was a certain glint to his eyes
And his apple showed her a certain sweetness all its own
Any girl would want to taste at least once or maybe twice
And Eve told Adam she must meet the Serpent now and then

Although Adam had known about the Serpent all along
And she'd told Adam she must meet the Serpent now and then
The nakedness of her honesty overwhelmed Eve
As Adam embarrassed by his own naked heart held her
Although even now he knew there was nothing he could do

12:00 Midnight-TBA

Their graven signs said, "Nevermore!"–
eleven men outside my door,
apace in beards and Roman gear–
And I could feel God growing near.

They said that God would come today,
and knock in His distinctive way;
they said that He would bring a friend,
together to announce the end.

Across the Water

Is this the land of the golden highways;
Is this the city of the jewelled dreams?
And what fire! What fire burns still brightly here?
Does the fire burn with heat or only light?

The sun from the water seems to ascend
The sky dripping with water and with fire,
While across the water silver towers shine
With their own cold fire against the heavens.

In the west is a dark rainbow some climb
Into that dark place across the water
To find only death in fading buildings,
Decaying fallen life outside the light.

And further east the earth swallows masses
Who follow the Prince of Darkness blindly
Into his dark world like Persephone,
All the while holding her torch high for light.

Where is the ferryman? Where the wild dog
With three heads, waiting to cross the water?
Over there, are there life giving flowers
Or only the dark across the water?

autumn scene
across
the water

from the beach
three black mast shapes
pierce the blazing
setting sun

chromatic
water flows still
here to there from
these dark holes

from the beach
they ask, "to where;
what dark corners,
what new worlds?"

temporal
darkness growing
pierced by fading
distant lamps:

from the beach
pinpoints dancing
recall the fall
setting sun.

Rendezvous

and another thing,
when you left
last time
why did you
not
set a definite
time to meet
again?

I know
your side was still
sore
and hurt
was yours
several ways
but the promise
was there
I thought
think
fail
to understand

There are people
I have known
say you won't
be back
say you spoke
a lie
a pass el
In fact

Rendezvous, page 2 of 2

        I thought
        you would
        come
        some time
        ago
        some where
        near;
        you said
        you would
        and I
        would know

        some indians said
        you came
        and left
        again
        never bothering
        to contact
        me
        saying you
        would come
        again

        How long is one thousand?

After the Magician: Before the Musicians

For about the space of half an hour in silence
I wait for the rite to begin, sipping my tea
Until the priest arrives at the altar with incense
And calls the seven trumpeters to play their part

The greatest show on earth or anywhere I know
Has only just begun and the house is packed:
I do not want to miss the end for anything
So I sit in silence rather than lose my place

Although I am awed by the special effects
And by the skilful staging I am waiting
Myself for the call for volunteers to come
Forth from the audience so I may play my part

Show me that show but give me that secret book
And give me that reed like a rod and let me see
The magic at work and show me that shining city
And show me also behind the scenes after the show.

I   (a)   Who are you?

       (b)   I have held many names
                   Been named many things
                   I am your friend
                   I am...
                   I am what you will.

                   Will you walk with me
                   In this garden?

       (a)   I trust you...
                   My trust is real
                   Really do trust you
                   More than I could trust
                   Anyone... almost

       (b)   Will you walk?

       (a)   I will.

II   It is so peaceful here–
                   So unlike
                   Reality should be...
                   What is this place?

       (b)   It is a land you do not know
                   You have travelled here before
                   And you will come again, yet
                   Nevermore
                   For here you have lived and called
                   Home
                   And here you shall return.

"Who are you?" page 2 of 3

III	You are
	In the magic garden
	You knew as a child
	Where people are born
	And die
	Here
	Old men seek
	Youth
	And leave, children
	Seeking wisdom.
IV	I am your brother
	Our father is one
	And the same
	Our minds...
V	In the garden
	Men first gained wings
	Lived below water
	And above
	The clouds.
	This garden
	Makes parachutists
	Of dandelion seeds;
	Fanciful ladies
	Of old green trees;
	A pirate's ocean of
	A creek's bend–
	A man of
	An ape

Who are you?" page 3 of 3

        VI   This magic garden
                    Can bring
                    Love
                    To Mankind.

These Eyes

Look through these eyes
and see what you will see:

He stands on the hill
looking
and sees the city
cluster of rainbow boxes
breathing demons
rising from brick caves
clutching at passersby.

Thought turns him
to the earth trail
to the forest beyond.

Look through these eyes
and see what you will see:

Below, a canvas forest
magic rock circles
incense burning
the forest raising roots
and creeping to shadows
of the hillside: hillside
embracing the forest.

Look through these eyes
and see what you will see:

A hand waves.
It removes the plastic city
and prunes the woven jungle
to trees.

These Eyes, page 2 of 2

> The hill stands alone
> a silent monument.
>
> He stands on the hill
> looking down.
>
> Look through these eyes
> and see what you will see:
>
> He stands looking
> on the hill
> plants growing creatures
> one side plain the other forest
> growing creatures
> In the peace of unmagic.
>
> He thinks
> and drops think to just one life
> growing creatures
> plants: thought.
>
> Look through these eyes
> and see what you will see:
>
> He stands on the hill
> looking
> and sees the city
> cluster of rainbow boxes
> breathing.
>
> Thought turns him around
> to the narrow earth trail
> to the forest.

after the flood

something happened at the market
in the light or in the air's feel
and her universe tipped slightly
'til the girl got carried away

vendor's table become rainbow
caught the girl's eye and drew her in
not like she had any control
bought the rainbow and took it home

something happened at the market
inside the girl and changed her world
not like she had any control
left the shadows became herself

in her window hung the rainbow
billboard for all the world to see
sighed relieved she could come out and live
unmasked and free to be herself

come from next door Christian said
how wonderful is your rainbow
hung so proudly in the window
as God's promise to flood no more

Like Omar's guests, I am star-scattered through the universe;
like the twelve tribes, I am gone into all the world and lost;
like all the stars, I am all around yet so far from you.

I reach out to you from everywhere and from nowhere,
hope you are whole and real as I reach with all of me
for you who can touch all my parts and gather them in.

For you who can make me whole as I have never done,
I reach out through all eternity and all longing,
but it seems that you, all star-scattered, have left yourself.

Life in a Bottle

The world softens perceptibly
in the soft focus of the snow
lacelike in the air around me.

I walk out with nowhere to go,
and I long for that perfect age
the softer focus seems to show.

As though the world, turned back a page,
returned me to a peerless time,
I seem to leave the modern rage.

I leave this age of hate and crime,
of death and hunger and abuse,
to enter snowfall's dream sublime.

For just a while I slip the noose
I feel around my neck and life,
as though the snow has set me loose.

Free for now from this world of strife
I am part of a soft vignette:
a portrait of some flawless life.

I long to find this place and yet
I know this dream can never be,
but what I've seen I'll not forget.

Flying

I think of David
on the verge of a ledge
a mile or more above
the green valley below

I think of David
fallen from the rock face
a broken-winged bird
helpless on that ledge

I think of David
out beyond the edge
pushed perhaps by Earle
or someone very like him

I think of David
high on mountain air
a bird in flight
soaring ever down

I think of Daedalus
at the edge of the sky
reaching for the sun
and Icarus far above

Some times of night the world seems far away
So like a life we dream to have some day,
While all around the mists obscure and hide
The world of man from man who would reside,
A spiral snail aloof among the dew
Of high rise grass and wait the reaper's shoe
That ends the day to leave behind crushed shell,
'Though where the snail has gone no one can tell.
And yet does not this snail become the mist
About a dream another world has kissed
With love and made by love to be its own
So that again the sower's seed is sown,
This time no reaper waiting to receive
Nor shell aspiral needed to deceive.

Do we each stand on our own shrinking line
Precariously grasping slim dash Earth,
Brief hyphen pausing between death and birth,
And wait to fall like needles from a pine?
Do we but separate front from the rear,
Beginning from the end and birth from death?
Can this be how our goodly book ended?
Shall ending periods become our fear?
We hold to this line while proving our worth
As grammarians wait our repentance
Until the hyphen becomes longer pause.
As hyphen I stand between death and birth
Awaiting not a point to end my sentence
But colon gates opened to my next clause.

On walking through the stacks of books in ordered rows,
For seven days, no more, no less, to move some mind,
Of thoughts in rows and racks awaiting those
Exciting days of freedom from the aisle's shut blind,
I stand and wonder waxlike whence my wicklife glows.
Is there a shelf somewhere reserved for me I'll find
All lined with rows and racks of lives come to a close
And Dewey signed to fit a row, to fit a kind?
This is shelf, is stacks - this loan of seven shadows
Ends in sunlight past the bright and glowing pillage,
Open books reflecting thought in golden billows;
Glowing fire, this wick the wax will turn to Life's page.
Loan oh a love like a bird on the wing which goes
Soaring this library bearing the burning age.

Last Call

Is this place taken; mind if I sit?

Time is on my side, so I listen:
Place to place, time to time, dark to dark,
Differing darkly, unknown in light,
He has sat, has shared my table, drunk,
Whispered as we moved from room to room,
Pointed, appointed places and times,
Told designs, places, plans, times and times,
Noted on some secret analogue
Men's comings, goings, times to come, all
Till watchless I asked myself the time:

The rest is over; the time is up,
He said, got up and, smiling, crossing
The bar, turned tender, served me one more

A world in the mirror
A face without end
A life time of furor
A time for a friend.

You are
It belongs to you
They are
It belongs to them
A Place
We are
Past tense of are
A place
A point in time
A method of comparison
The number 2
Indicates motion
Also or excessively

the grey people linger in the periphery
until you turn and see all the usual colours
while light's magic creates rainbow shaded people
grey beneath but hidden by the shimmering light

not red and yellow black and white but shadow grey
against the natural prism of a world that was
in the periphery where dark shadows menace
while dreams become the only world there is turned grey

grey as the sidewalks and concrete city buildings
grey people everywhere hidden in plain sight
their peripheral world overcomes and subverts
people not noticing grey creatures on the side

at dusk I notice in shop windows as I pass
tucked away in the glass beside me something grey
follows me wherever I walk the city streets
I reflect the grey creature following is me

Twenty Four

Paper dot black velvet
Between grey shades and silence
Centre spark blue gingham
Between grey shades soon silence

Time
Flutters on the wind
Like lacedrops melting
To a greener shade.

Time
Bundles white blankets
About a new world
Swaddling lace cocoon.

Man
Sees not the treasure
Of a trove in lace
Hung by drifting time.

Focus Time

Thinking back on spring
something in summer
sun betrays the scars

summer colour fades
falling leaves and rust
fulfilling something

new lives born from old
seeds as petals fall
winter promised spring

Passing Time

We walk together
in the solitude
of silent moments

our small eternity

besides you have to admit we're good together
settled naked in the bed beside each other
after the earth has moved and we melded
amongst the sweat and moaning and small death
you have to admit you and I come
together as you ride me and I you
until we fall exhausted still touching each other
our love never ending in our small eternity

The lamp in the ceiling will burn out soon,
Sending the room into darkness
And groping and groping, I'll cross the gloom
Seeking the switch against the blindness.

The carpet below me will be a bed,
Bedroom and home until warning
The blue room around calls, and I'll be led
From lamp into sunshine morning.

Bolex

There is no sound in this black and white world
missing even the whir of the Bolex
drawing in what it sees without comment
images to flicker on future walls
projecting a past world in black and white

A boy and girl climb the wooded dirt path
beside a green lake somewhere far below
followed by mother coming up behind
saying words now lost somewhere in the past
and father unseen behind the Bolex

A girl runs down a road in Viet Nam
screaming in silence as napalm burns her
while a newsman weeps behind his Bolex
while the world weeps at this black and white scene
knows things can no longer be black and white

The car door opens over and over
while the girl and boy follow each other
out of the car out of the car like magic
black and white and silent without ending
controlled by the man behind the Bolex

Over and over passenger jets crash
twin towers into reasons for new wars
while the New York artist in his loft makes
moving images with an old Bolex
knowing nothing is truly black and white

The boy sails a kite gently in the sky
as he runs through the fields eternally
looped slo-mo over and over again
the man with the Bolex keeping the dark
just out of reach where it can't touch this boy

Anne Frank writes her diary in an attic
knows the men in uniforms will come soon
bearing death for her family and her
writes with no Bolex to tell this story
as the attic closes in on her life

A girl on the cabin's porch is reading
while across the meadow a deer watches
her dad in the doorway filming this girl
her thoughts far away in a dark attic
with another girl about her own age

Unfeeling uniformed men with guns watch
people undress for the waiting showers
then enter a dark room they'll never leave
while the gas stacks naked bodies like logs
all shot for the record with a Bolex

On a sunny day somewhere in the west
a boy chases a dog through prairie grass
while the man with the Bolex follows him
pleased to catch the fire of the summer sun
above this boy and dog in black and white

The eastern sun sits low in the sky
where rockets explode and a city burns
while across the way festive crowds gather
cheering with joy at fireworks in the dusk
while an antique Bolex records it all

There must be birdsong in the fields and woods
yet there is no sound in these images
no colour among the black and white fields
where light and dark are given equal weight
the Bolex records but never judges

Above Japan three men wait the moment
Little Boy falls from the bomb bay
silence all around them like death calling
then fire takes innocence out of their world
while The Great Artiste's Bolex captures all

In a sunlit world without sound or colour
a boy and girl seem to live forever
dream of love floating across perfect fields
but it stops to leave a single image
where a spark spreads until nothing is left

Snapshot: December 17, 2013

in this black sky there is no noon sun
the dark smothers all sense of daylight
silence has fallen across the land
a pall of smoke forecasts coming death
sirens wail against the still quiet air

spreading across the land like cancer
the shadow of some black predator
hushed hunter seeking some final end
and the flames! Oh bright flames growing
sun fallen to earth to devour all

in the heavens an ancient man hangs
the shadow spreading to take him in
fingers of fire reaching to take him
an ancient man hangs waiting in hopes
an angel will pluck him from this sky

the holy choir below is silent
the seasonal concert is cancelled
the angel voices lost in the smoke
the inferno spreading like brimstone
this is no occasion to rejoice

out of the dark and flames sparks of hope
stars against that terrific sky spread
everywhere light against the darkness
against the fire's eager appetite
human souls holding back the darkness

Highrise fire destroys city block
Winter 2013: Kingston, Ontario

Conspiracy

Time drifts secretly, filtering through the hovering smoke
Above people who listen raptly to an old man who raves
Of eternal life entwined with youthful exuberance and pleasure.
And Time, hanging as Damocles' sword over them, laughs.
For this possessèd old man has led them, has pushed them
To the precipice which must be their inevitable goal.
They, these wisdom bound peasants, are trapped
Misled by devious Time and his disciple.
Thinking to avoid in their deceitful way
Times compatriot...
DEATH

hell is a coal mine
workers buried deep below ground
become black as coal

Life Underground

If you live underground,
you don't see the light;
you don't see nothing at all.
Yes, that's what they told me,
and what I believed,
until I took my great fall.

At first I was blinded
by stars glaring bright:
leaders of light but not fire.
Like a shadow I followed
fads and illusions,
and saw myself living high.

And I followed the crowd
into the darkness,
and I saw nothing at all.
I saw not the darkness
around all my life --
how much I'd put on the shelf.

Then I turned from the light
just for a moment
and found myself underground.
I saw fire burn brightly
and light seared my soul:
I felt myself falling in.

Life Underground, page 2 of 2

When I found my focus
the world seemed unreal:
my idols had lost their sheen.
So I walked beyond light
and felt myself falling
into the fire's salvation.

They say:

If you live underground,
you don't see the light;
you don't see nothing at all.
But my fire burned brightly
and light seared my soul
deep in the fire's salvation.

When the sea has passed me by
And my towel's lain to dry
None shall even know my name
Sand and I shall be the same.

How Do I Remember

I remember the Lac des Arcs A-frame
our big old house on first and main in Olds
the home we built above the studio
the Kimberly house on a mountainside
Sylvan Lake's house and the cottage behind
a quiet street near the hill in Red Deer
our houses in Bowness and Calgary

You were always there

I remember drives across Alberta
photo shoots of prize beef and palominos
northern oil rig photo shoots and picnics
Sikorsky and glass-bubble Bell choppers
Banff and Radium and The Cariboo
half-tracks on the Columbia Ice Fields
steam-trains to O'Flaherty's in Ottawa

You were always there

it was always the waiting was hardest
but we knew you would choose the time to go
first there were celebrations to be had
your birthdays and your anniversary
you had life and love still to give us all
the waiting was hardest and yet the best

You were always there

How Do I Remember, page 2 of 2

      how do I remember you and not weep
      you who had always been our strong centre
      even now your shadow walks at my side
      and I feel your hand holding mine each day
      still you walk with me and you comfort me
      You light my path even when it's most dark
      for me your memory will always live

      You will always be here in my heart

                            Phyllis May MacKenzie née O'Flaherty
                            (May 29, 1920 - October 14, 2013)

Time and the Prophet

Borne on the storm,
Father before
Followed the ledge -
Thunder his foe,
Lightning his load,
Upward the peaks.
Ever the wind,
Searching for peace
Over the clouds.

Born of the storm.
I am the door
Hung on the edge -
You are my foe,
(What is my load?)
Climbing the peaks.
Ever the wind,
Promising peace
Over the clouds.

Bee

Rose in sunshine opens up,
Red caressing way to pass—
Read the printed petals first.

Enter roses while ye may,
Deep in red enjoy a day—
Beware the nightly closing.

Tree

All life moves
Sun high
Tree green darkens

Bare arms reach
Pale sky
Lean arms beseech

Skeleton
Grey sky
Bone white blanket

The tree sits
Warm sky
Speckled frog world.

The Cutter

Scythe a swath across the sky
Expanse of snow the runners

Dash curved before us dusky
Buffalo enfolding all

Woodstove warmth to Eastward fade
Us and black the jingling beast

One Last Move

She stands and waits in silence at Death's door
bathed in grey shades of the impending dusk
waits until he opens the door at last
then smiles at him and walks into the mist
toward one more wonderful adventure

There is a man at the gate in soft robes
bathed in light as she appears from the haze
says he is Peter and she says Phyllis
has tea with him then leaves the light behind
seeking one more wonderful adventure

Phyllis walks between worlds and balances
never quite in one or the other and knows
soon she must decide to stay or to go
she knows it's been decided she must go
but not before just one more adventure

Phyllis teeters on that thin taut wire
between worlds waiting until she is ready
she has always decided and now will decide
when the time is right to cross that thin line
that transom where her new home waits for her

There is no loaded van for her to meet
baggage to unpack or chores remaining
but still she hangs on and waits a bit longer
smiles and has tea and eyes the door opening
to just one more wonderful adventure

>   Phyllis May MacKenzie née O'Flaherty
>   (May 29, 1920 - October 14, 2013)

Phase Shift

I am a slim shadow adrift in this packed room
slightly out of phase in time but enough for now
not visible to others though I do see them

a slim shadow crossing peripheral vision
a thought not admitted a sight not remembered
the outsider in the room full of insiders

in this room unseen and unheard I touch each one
they shiver and remember my shadow and voice
for a brief moment a slim shadow becomes real

they fear some darker shadow will someday find them
sensing the slim shadow in the room they shiver
feel the chill breeze as a shadow falls out of phase

Behind

Who are they? Where are they?

Turn! No one there!
Walk on slowly; afraid.
Terrified of one behind.

Driving in peace.
Those headlights behind–is it?
Yes! Following; following.

Strange they follow only sometimes...

Silent Shadows

Walking through rooms:
Empty rooms we all walk.
Oh what room is this?
Oh what door is this?
Oh where does it lead me?

Walking through these rooms:
Silent shadows
Say someone's here,
Someone's here
In this empty room -
In this echo room.

Where are you now?
What is your name now?
In this shadow box
Are we all alone?
Where do you lead me?

Other Winds

There are other winds
in the west
I have not yet felt.

They are there in wait
for the unwary
travelling in the dark.

They lurk in the shadows
of the Rockies
like gullies and ravines.

Their disguise is perfect
shadows among shadows
growing daily darker there.

Their disguise is perfect
whispering winds
among the mountain breezes.

One day I know I shall enter
the wrong dark ravine
meet the wrong dark wind.

Beware, cold Wind, the heat of day;
The eye that cuts your blade away.

Take all the dark can give this eve;
Yet watch lest dawn shall you bereave.

Both day and dusk we walk to you;
A friend and yet a passing view.

Red edge of dawn shall be your bed;
Cut now, frail breeze, your line of red.

Beware then, Wind, the burning sky;
Beware the blaze of one man's eye.

The Girl

The voices are there hidden in the night
where the girl can hear their every word
hidden behind corners and whispering
secrets along the street and in the trees

She shivers in the darkness and moves on
knowing the shadows follow and whisper
not only secrets but darker threats
all in languages only she understands

Somewhere near an owl's hollow hoot calls her
her name echoes off the city's hard walls
cats' wails follow in a bitter harmony
the girl only half understands but fears

The street falls silent but the girl hears still
shadows whispering darkly toward her
the hush following her every step
she falling into ever deeper dark

Sometimes the girl hears footsteps behind her
she turns to look but sees only the darkness
she sees the shadows slide along the walls
she shivers in the darkness and moves on

There is no sky behind the ink of night
the moon hides behind a black mask of clouds
someone has broken the streetlight bulbs
the voices are there hidden in the night

The Girl, page 2 of 5

        She shivers in the darkness and moves on
        shadows move slowly along the dark walls
        shadows whisper dark threats only she hears
        she shivers and moves on through the darkness

        Somewhere far away a siren shrieks out
        the siren bounces lightly off the walls
        The girl hears only voices that follow
        she hears only the whispers in the dark

        A far away siren meets the darkness
        the wail underscores a doowop song
        owl and cat harmonize with the siren
        the girl hears but only half understands

        The girl is alone in the darkest night
        a darkest night hides deep inside the girl
        there is no escape from the voices' whispers
        there is no escape from the creeping dark

        Somewhere near an owl's hollow hoot calls her
        an owl in the city how strange she thinks
        her name bounces off hard walls into black
        cat's wails follow her name into the dark

        The girl hears voices no other can hear
        she hears and she understands dark whispers
        threats in the night touch the girl deep within
        hide behind corners and whisper to her

The Girl, page 3 of 5

The dark grows thicker to smother the girl
not ink now the dark becomes living tar
the girl is wrapped in a black tar blanket
from somewhere the girl hears a siren call

The Voices are there hidden in the night
she shivers in the darkness and moves on
somewhere near she hears an owl's hollow call
the street falls silent but the girl hears still

Sometimes the girl hears footsteps behind her
she shivers in the darkness and moves on
there is no sky behind the ink of night
somewhere far away a siren calls her

Night's dark blanket scares her only a while
deep in her heart she feels new warmth growing
she drowns in night's warm comforting embrace
falling into deep sleep the siren wakes her

Fear releases the girl and blankets the warmth
in her heart is only the darkness she fears
in the night there is nobody to save her
there is only the shadows and the song

A scream slices the dark startling the girl
a scream seems to come from her own body
nobody hears nobody hears but her
she turns toward the darkness and moves on

The Girl, page 4 of 5

Somewhere in the night a doowop song plays
dark harmonies draw her into darkness
the dark rhythm carries past some threshhold
carries the girl toward dark beyond night

The voices are there hidden in the night
where the girl can hear their every word
and shivers in the darkness and moves on
and knows the shadows follow and whisper

Shadows whisper from deep in dark corners
secrets told on the street and in the trees
not only secrets but darker threats
told in languages only she understands

The girl is alone in the dark crying
nobody hears nobody knows but her
the girl follows a sound through the darkness
from somewhere she hears a doowop melody

Dark voices whisper to her through the night
threats in the night touch the girl deep within
somewhere far away a siren shrieks out
somewhere near she feels something dark approach

She sees only shadows hears only the song
nobody hears nobody knows but her
She shivers in the darkness and moves on
shadows follow slowly along dark walls

The Girl, page 5 of 5

The girl hears voices no other can hear
she hears and she understands dark whispers
there is no escape from the whispered voices
there is no escape from the creeping dark

The doowop music draws the girl deeper
dark harmonies pull her toward darkness
the girl walks deeper into the darkness
there is no escape from the creeping dark

The voices are there hidden in the night
the girl hears but cannot escape them
hidden behind corners and whispering
secrets through the trees and along the street

The scream echoes louder in the darkness
there is no escape from the creeping dark
there is no escape from screams in the night
the girl has lost her way in the darkness

Shadows move slowly along the dark walls
She shivers in the darkness and moves on
knows the shadows follow her and whisper
whisper dark threats that only she can hear

Something in the night reaches deep in her
she shivers and walks into the darkness
she drowns in night's warm comforting embrace
the girl falls into perfect sleep to dream

The sun shines brightly from clear blue skies
threatening voices and dark shadows hide
the girl is at peace in a perfect day
far away a doowop song fills the air

A flower opened this morning–
Smile at me sunshine,
Oh smile, for I am just a child,
Face filled with dewdrops.

Trip

Radio blares
softly
enhancing road bumps.

We move
to a destination
where smooth roads soothe
and silence radio sounds.

I live
He said
Affirming fact
Proving
Once more he was right
And
    He was happy.

Communion

Friend
I said to him and he would not listen
But stood aloof with fear in his sad eyes
Come
I beckoned him and he would not approach
Becoming a statue of that he was
Look
I said to him and his eyes averted
To an empty corner across the room
Friend
I said and held out my hand to him
And his eyes brightened
Come
I beckoned and threw a true smile to him
And he moved to me
Look
I said to him and showed him friendship
And his smile was real

Hymn

Signs of sunshine reach each corner as flowers gather dew;
sing your songs of sunny weather and we shall gather too.

Playing Tag

A friend came up as I walked in the garden,
Oh Friend, he spoke, how come you are here?
I turned - Is it in your soul to ask me why
The birds fly? A butterfly plays tag there;
Ask him why play! Present games become air,
Anticipating a new breath. You are the sigh
It will touch to win this game. Give a tear
For butterfly and me and go home free: Your
Self.

Soaring

The soul is a nest
Enfolding three birds.
One is flight.
One is night.
One is death.
What hand will take
The darker bird?

Lesson 68

As the proverbial birds in the bush
Reach air, one flies, one glides, one is in the hand.
"Is Death in this picture?" cries the teacher,
"And what of the three birds of ancient lore,
Should there be less or should there be more?"

Flight Training

Link trainer hands
Fly and soar and swoop and dive
Happy flights around the world
All at the end of an arm.
Think where you could fly
If you were free!

Fly

A spring day whisks me away in its whims,
And bubbled now in a city proof sky–
In a bright ringed jewel lookout–
Wind, I ride over metaphors of grass
And half phrased in the beauty of it all
Draw a simile on this sun greened day,
As a hush of butterflies flutter by;
And I, rough drafting flower thoughts aside
Sun with my pad and toy with my hover craft.

Earth that is Me breathes every Moon

Indentured swelling fading flooding
Canalled and diked terra firma I
Adrift unremitting awash washed
Within without and yet withal sea
Rising falling moon bound of for by
Earth that is me breathes every moon

Positive Café

In the café, he sits alone as though waiting
a fixture at his table by the inside wall

there's no obvious invitation to others
no call to visit this private space where he sits

he sits in solitary peace outside this room
not of this world yet seems to understand it all

there is no wall around him to keep others out
there is no obvious invitation either

the invitation comes from somewhere deep within
where his heart smiles and says welcome to all who come

in the café others come to him where he sits
content to simply be while others seek something

like Christ or The Buddha or any simple monk
he is a magnet sharing his calm with the world

A strange word
Overtakes being
With passion of the ages.

Love.

Love

Like leaves in the wind
Our lives entwine Love's branches
And our world grows green.

Earth

First robin of spring
Crocus rising from the ground—
Such is your beauty.

against white snow fields
prairie crocus purple hints
spring cannot be far

Your mind and mine meet:
What fire! What thunder! What life!
World meets world–spring rain

baseball metaphors crack
right off the bat into stands
filled with eager ears

Child Paints

These people
Breathe flowers from their noses
Their fingers are flowers too
And spring wraps around them.

How pretty these people are
With lives filled with flowers
And sunshine.

Winter's artist's hand,
Sticklike gopher in the field–
Long black lines sun paints.

Summer Somewhere

I've dreamed of a summer somewhere
Where the sun is always high,
Shining through the clear air
Above both you and I.

I seek all starlight,
I seek the sun–
Oh summer somewhere,
You are the one.

As you walk out in the meadow,
Go to brook and go to sea,
Sailing as the birds go
Sailing, sailing free.

And I watch you in the forest,
Best of woman, best of light,
Flower that gives no rest
Shining in the night.

Oh summer somewhere,
Oh where are you–
Sing me your lovesong,
None less will do.

I've dreamed of a summer somewhere
Where the sun is always high,
Shining through the clear air
Around both you and I.

I remember the roses growing wild
on bushes behind the old wood garage
beside the alley dividing back yards

wild pink roses set against dark green leaves
each a fine balance of five soft petals
and the universe a flawed mandala

I remember that back yard on First Street
a savannah of deep waving wild grass
the dog would bounce through chasing shadows

the cat rediscovering lion past lives
crouching through that wild grass after prey
while we caught butterflies and bees in jars

I remember my uncle chasing us
around the hedge and the disused capped well
pretending my cousin and I were too fast

autumn leaf-filled ditches were our playground
cottonwood like snow covering our street
the wide verandah becoming our stage

I remember moving day as adventure
and us hiding in empty kitchen cupboards

Autumnlike before our springdance
Leaves whisper soft to the ground

(Death before life)

Whitelimbs bare dancing the snow
Fallenlife 'til wintering

(Life after death)

We in duskyroom dancing
Pause a moment to softly touch.

Autumnlike before our springdance
Leaves whisper soft to the ground

Whitelimbs bare dancing the snow
Fallenlife 'til wintering

We in duskyroom dancing
Pause a moment to softly touch.

Light

Remember today,
Always
As it was before
We woke
Long past memories;
It is morning.

Christina, mind child living
Free as a thought, and freer.
She is the poet/writer.

Christina is a love thought,
Recording sadness in youth–
Showing beauty in sadness.

And building new styles of love.

Two Girls

They smiled across the room
Wearing voices of friends
As overcoats against
My everdamp presence there.
"Hi".

I nodded vaguely...
Alone.

Oak

she is uncertain how she came to this wood
surrounding her with shards of light and shadows
dancing spirits drawing her out of the light

her eyes turn to the clearing bathed in day's last light
slim shadows spoked toward the oak at the centre
and him
        a small man crouched at the great oak's base

taking this man is only the beginning
his hand in hers she flees the grasping shadows
determined to make the man hers for a while

A Romance I

Guinevere

life is but a faery tale:
Castle near,
Guinevere.
Lancelot, I ride to meet
My fair lady.

O what a magic scene this is:
In the sun
Questing one;
Through the world to seek and find
My fair lady.

A Romance II

The Quest

I am Galahad and you are Rapunzel,
Sleeping Beauty and Snow White; damsel let down your hair:
I alone slay dragons between breaths;
Beauty-seeker seeking you, O perfect one,
And swashbuckling to win your heart, the heart of a pure maiden.

I shall Errol Flynn my way into your heart—
Woman worthy of battle, woman worthy of love—
Fight pirates, slay dragons, foil villains;
Show the world my bravery, O steadfast love,
And you shall be my only love, at least until tomorrow.

A Romance III

The Grail
(Tiresias at twenty five)

I come and go, crossing and searching
This warm fog feel of you Universe
Like a Blind Man in search of the Grail,
Galahad again, and you England,
Mapped by blind fingers feeling, flowing—
You come and go as the oceans flow,
Shrouding Sun and England in fog thoughts:
Hazy Grail, how often were you found,
Unseen by nightly wrestling searchers
Expecting more of the Universe?

A Romance IV

Changes

Long now have I loved you as a woman,
Person, self and part-of-me (a thralldom
Built on softness). Roses have such power:
Who can pass and fail to pause in wonder
That The Garden yields such fiery beauty?
What rose is there I can bear you, as Love,
Would not admit your superior art?
Rose petals conceal as much as show Rose:
Long have I known you in the day, but
Still your spirit baffles me at nightfall.

A Romance V

Careering

It seems he works all the time now
And there is none of the old love,
Sense that he is always with me,
Galahad guarding my each move–
But thou, O Quest, he worships thee!

But still the bird comes to sing me
How Lancelot and Galahad
Seek the Grail that fits like a glove;
He loves me, yet still I am sad,
Sitting, wondering how this can be.

A Romance VI

Affirmation

We were one, youthful bathers in the sun;
We were young, water babies - two come one.

Woman mine, like a melon ripening
(Time Improves), like a flower opening.

Could there be any modern photograph
Could in time capture true your youthful laugh?

Here we stand, youthful bathers in the sun;
Here we stand, aged shrivels - two yet one.

You are she, handsome woman that I wed–
Beauty born, beauty aged, come to bed.

A Romance VII

Till Death Doe

I am alone now, yet I know you are near;
your sleep is but a lull in our conversation,
a hush before our next words will be spoken;
your eyes are closed only to what you will not see,
and your ears only to what you will not hear.

Life has become to you a simple parlour game
which you finally understand and turn away,
seeking new conversations and new games to play;
and yet, I feel Love waiting for me to catch up,
making this moment the pause we take between breaths.

Masts

The trees in the harbour smile as I pass
And harbour their secret leaves in the grass.

Girl on a Swing

Hung by slim threads from the sky
she swings back into my arms
and I hold her there briefly
but she swings away from me
ever up toward the sun
pauses still against the sky
seeks some distant horizon

then falls back into my arms
where I hold her so briefly
until she swings out from me
up toward her distant dream
perhaps to once again pause
and swing back into my arms
or forever fly from me

Randolph

And sometimes he,
My Randolph, seems to say
In growing,
"Look, I'm only passing through
Like a stranger."

On rainy days,
He moves through the kitchen
Like a myth,
Leaving muddy memories
Of his passing.

And in sunshine,
He runs in the back and
Out the front,
Leaving silent echoings
Of his passing.

But sometimes his,
My Randolph's, eyes are mine,
Whispering,
"I may be just passing through
But I'm with you."

trapeze

She swings
toward me and away
afraid of falling
to the sawdust below
yet daring the flight
outward and upward
hands outstretched toward me
then swinging back once more
away from me
she swings

Flirtation

I shall unwrap your eyes with mine,
Loosening bowed lids,
And shall remove the gift within–
Carefully caress.

Yet where shall you be wandering
While I'm in your eyes
(Admiring wealth, not plundering
Cities of your mind)?

See here the gates and enter now,
Enter as sunshine
And conquer all, and bid them bow–
Provinces of mine.

meeting

she jumps me, she jives me, she drives me
passes by me, deep soul kisses me, sucks
my heart up out of my mouth deep into her

we talk across a table and beer, and my soul—
I see my soul shine somewhere in her eyes
I see and know as she is now mine I am hers

we are as naked in this public place as later
we will be undressed, the taste of each other
like sacred manna feeding our now united souls

naked words pass between us, our eyes hearing
bare truths as they pass between us, our eyes
locked on naked words, our shared souls passing

between us eternity opens up and momentarily
we are one within eternity and know we share
not some eternal truth at all, but each other

Love song.
Lovesong,
Flash your fire across the sky
Etch her name in every eye:
Flaming.
Flaming,
Like an ancient tree she burns
Leaving roots whence she returns:
Flower.
Flower,
Flaring flower in my mind
Etching pages meant to bind:
Love's song.
Love's song,

if she is a goddess
no fire and brimstone here
no thunder and lightning
no scarring words or threats

if she is a goddess
hers is gentle power
her strength comes through wisdom
her guidance words of love

if she is a goddess
she is the calm centre
she brings love and caring
she brings gentle guidance

If she is a goddess
she carries light with her
and comfort when needed
and she is a goddess

My love for you shall remain quiet and soft and firm as the Earth itself and as eternal as the heavens above. Although I may not always say it, you are that bright star in my sky that for so long I have not noticed is the one star that guides me as I move through my life. Thank you simply for being exactly who you are.

I Would Photograph You

I would photograph you in just that way,
you reclining among the windblown grain,
the sun winnowing its light through your hair,
your cotton summer dress soft in its light.

You would be resting there in the sunlight
gazing up the hill at that warm farm home
inviting you to come when you're ready
like that shining city you see in dreams.

I would add colour to this photograph,
clover perhaps or daisies in the breeze,
and bright paint on that old grey house and barn,
and add a bright print to your cotton dress.

I would photograph you in just that way,
lit by sunlight in a world of flowers
where songbirds sing and the sun seeks you out
but, most of all, I would photograph you.

Hidden in back alleys they kiss; the lovers
Hiding their love in the night...
Just as lovers hide their secret kisses
In the back alleys of the world–
So they hide their secret thoughts
In the back alleys of the brain.
And some secret thoughts never reach the love mate.

If a thousand thousand poets' clever
Words enshrined their loves as art, then
Surely all the metaphors are taken.

I may speak of stars or roses never
Seen before, speak of beauty without peer,
Say they pale when placed by your pure light.

Art and nature leave me without insight,
Images or words.

          If words may seem clear,
They remain just words, and you are real.

You may be that star, that rose, and may be
all the poets write about, but I feel
You: your heart, your soul, your warmth when near me.

You are.

          That is enough for me to see
Your best metaphor is reality.

Red String

A direct line from your breast
where it rests beneath my hand
links my heart and soul to yours
like we have been joined always,

the red string on our ankles
tying us eternally
in a love we both had felt
and sought throughout our lives,

a tension drawing us here
to this place where our hearts meet
and I lay by your soft form
and cup your breast in my hand.

soft my angel sleeps

soft you settle into my chest and become part of me
a warmth next to my heart that, for the moment at least,
completes me and fulfills some deep longing within me

feeling your body warm next to mine, I am completed
and whole, more than a man and joined in a greater whole,
the warmth of you fulfilling me in our private Eden

beside me, your sleeping face is peaceful and angelic,
and I could believe that you had fallen from Heaven
especially to fill my arms and waiting heart

soft your skin nestles into mine like a sweet smile
I recall the touch of your fingers gentle as a breeze
and you asking me, "am I hurting you?"

soft you settle into my chest and take me into you
and I begin a journey toward some sweet eternity
this angel walking beside me, and I can only hope

Flight Risk

Her soaring thoughts bear her up on gossamer and
hard realities, her wings carry me with her
to another place only her mind can take mine
and with her I soar upward as I've never soared.

"I am a flight risk teetering on some slight edge,
ready to flee at a moment's notice," she says.

There is a small brown bird, a finch, unpresuming,
tourists buy in cages from asian street sellers
because her singing is so sweet, so beautiful
and, before the tourist reaches home, the bird dies.

What cage shall I build and of what material
will not forever stop her soaring singing heart?
How clip those wings of fantasy and hold her in
never again to soar so high and I soar too?

What risk in flight is so great it must be taken
away and the blue sky blocked from view and the wings
never again to soar nor that brown bird's sweet song heard,
its heart stopped at the bottom of some bamboo cage?

She is a flight risk, no doubt, but that's the tension,
the beauty of her as something in her flies high
escaping to some realm all her own and sometimes,
just sometimes carrying me with her to rapture.

I would take the risk to fly away in her wake
and if she turned away and flew beyond my reach
would still have known the joy of glorious flight
while somewhere in the wild a small brown bird still sings.

"I am a flight risk teetering on some slight edge,
ready to flee at a moment's notice," she says.

The Uncaged Bird

It's letting her go that's most difficult
releasing her and knowing she'll fly home
but knowing sometimes pigeons don't return
knowing that she's free to fly her own course

It's letting her go that's most difficult
releasing the hawk from your wrist to fly
into some unknown sky and distant heart
land she may decide to make her new home

It's letting her go that's most difficult
freeing this songbird from her bamboo cage
to fly perhaps to yet another cage
or else to sing for all the world to hear

It's letting her go that's most difficult
never placing her in a cage at all
watching as she flies off to somewhere else
never knowing if she'll come back to me

mostly I'm missing you
not because I love you
although of course I do
or that your love for me
is not as I love you

mostly I'm missing you
because we share so much
when we talk late at night
and explore common views
that only we can share

mostly I'm missing you
just when you are not here
and I can't see your face
and I can't hear your voice
because you are not here

mostly I'm missing you
not because I love you
although of course I do
but simply for the space
that's left when you are gone

                    you live here

it seems you have been here all along
so when I notice you
                    it's not strange
you're just there as you always have been

there are bits of you strewn through the house
fall leaves adding colour to my world
where otherwise there might be none at all

sometimes I see you or hear your voice
you live here
              so long after you called
announcing the end of everything

yet still remnants of you remain here
an old toothbrush
                    a clock you gave me
our music
           our places
                  bits of you

I bear your mark and it doesn't fade
I feel you beside me
                  I hear your voice
I see you there at the edge of sight

can true love be erased from the heart
how can I answer what I don't know
how can I know if I did love you

I do know you have stayed here with me
long after you told me we should part
and I see and hear you
                    you live here

Even when you are not here with me
I sense you just outside of eyesight
You stand there soft in my memory
like the warming touch of the sunshine
caressing my cheek on some park bench
one autumn day barely remembered
yet somehow vivid as yesterday.

I am warmed by your soft memory
even when you are not here with me
but filling my heart with thoughts of you
filling my mind with the essence of you
filling my being with love for you
caressing my cheek like sunshine
until I can be with you once more.

Beyond Convergence: The Whistle Dying

Midnight rolls on down the line
Incisive: No Coyote this,
Howling darker prairie worlds
In passing sullen rumble;

Gone the whistle mistlike spread
Across the land, the fire breath
Steamborne passing Manitou:
Type of Gods we dream no more.

outside the office
life is vast but without order
here he knows his place

It seems so long ago; now
I've walked this white line,
It seems my whole life,
Balancing on the line.
(two dimension puppet show
but for what audience?)
There must have been a time,
Young and eager past time,
I walked both sides freely
And left the painted line
A trolley for white canes
Of older men gone blind.
But that was long ago,
Before I saw the line
As success, as a train
Following the blinding
White glare of the old line
I have joined.

Edge

I've been standing in the cold falling rain
hearing the pulse of its heart beat down
seeing the dark images in its shadows
like the visions of ancient prophets
and I have seen that I stand in the gutter
between the edges between worlds apart
between gay and straight between rich and poor
between capital and commune between woman and man
between every possible polarity you can dream
looking at those edges not from the other side
but from somewhere between which is nowhere
and I have disappeared

don't get me wrong and don't get it twisted
it may after all have been only a dream
it may be I have seen nothing at all
and there was nothing at all to see in the rain
nothing but a magic shadow-show played in a box
lit by sun and moon against silhouettes of rain
around which we phantom figures come and go
the rain falling like knives slicing the dark
to create worlds then wash them away in a flash
lit by lightning that wakes me with a start

the words of the prophets echo down the centuries
truth grown tired and worn until the words are only dust
choking off the little breath we gasp to survive
the uncertain future we have created for ourselves
and in the words we hear echoing somewhere distant
the pulsing of a heartbeat pounding like a hammer
and feel that pulse drawing us out toward the edge

Edge, page 2 of 7

I've lived too long too near the edge
stood too close to where it happens
seen what I should not have seen
and heard it all and hear it still
in living dreams I cannot escape

there are people living on the edge
it is true, I have seen them there
clinging to the thin line between them
and the other side of their reality
have stood behind them as they clung
hopeless noses pressed to some window
to some place they could not enter
and I have stayed in the shadows
knowing they would not see me there

I have seen
I have seen
I have seen the best minds of my generation
and they are the same as those seen long ago
and they are not just America
and they are not destroyed after all
nor drag themselves through black streets
but stand waiting arm in arm to hold firm
against that rough beast, its hour come round
as it slouches unrelenting through every street
seeking some holy land and preordained birth

don't get me wrong and don't get it twisted
many people strive for high ideals
and everywhere life is full of heroism
but what does it matter in the end
what does it matter who is hero and who not
when it may after all be only a dream
and there was nothing at all to see but the rain
through which we come and go like phantoms
as the rain falls like knives slicing the dark
impulse of winter midnight streetlight rain
creating worlds that wash away in a flash
of lightning that wakes us with a start

there are people
cries in the wilderness
there are people
cries in the wilderness
there are people gathered in the streets
flooding the streets of every town and city
cries in the wilderness of grey streets
gathered with pens and with pitchforks
crying for justice all over this land
men and women standing arm in arm everywhere
warning of danger, crying out a warning
cries in the wilderness

Edge, page 4 of 7

    in the room the people come and go
    talking of what they have seen out there
    but they don't go out there and they
    and they don't do anything to stop it
    in the dark in the room the people watch
    in the silence in the room they listen
    and drown awash in flickering images
    and drown in the battle's sound and fury
    across the universe and back again
    and still falls the rain like helpless tears

    he stands in the shadows of the evening rain
    the gentle rain that falls for years
    just a little boy standing in the rain
    and rain keeps falling like helpless tears
    still falls the rain with a sound like the pulse
    the pulse of the heart that is changed to the hammer-beat
    and rain keeps falling like helpless tears
    the boy disappears

    still I feel the heartbeat beating underneath every thing
    the pulse of the heart that is changed to the hammer-beat
    the pulse of the heart that hammers out love
    the pulse of the heart that hammers out danger
    the pulse of the heart that hammers out a warning
    the pulse of the heart that hammers out hatred
    while the rain keeps falling like helpless tears
    while the best among us lose all conviction
    while the worst grow full of passionate intensity
    and the heartbeat pulses between every thing

Edge, page 5 of 7

        don't get me wrong and don't get it twisted
        it may after all have been only a dream
        it may be I have seen nothing at all
        and there was nothing at all to see in the rain
        nothing but a magic shadow-show played in a box
        lit by sun and moon against silhouettes of rain
        around which we phantom figures come and go
        the rain falling like knives slicing the dark
        to create worlds then wash them away in a flash
        lit by lightning that wakes me with a start

        I've lived too long too near the edge
        stood too close to where it happens
        seen what I should not have seen
        and heard it all and hear it still
        in living dreams I cannot escape

        the words of the prophets echo down the centuries
        truth grown tired and worn until the words are only dust
        choking off the little breath we gasp to survive
        the uncertain future we have created for ourselves
        and in the words we hear echoing somewhere distant
        the pulsing of a heartbeat pounding like a hammer
        and feel that pulse drawing us out toward the edge

Edge, page 6 of 7

        surely some revelation is at hand
        cries in the wilderness between the lines
        this is the way the world ends
        cries in the wilderness between the lines
        this is the way the world ends
        cries in the wilderness between the lines
        this is the way the world ends
        as we stand waiting arm in arm to hold firm
        against that rough beast, its hour come round
        as it slouches unrelenting through every street
        seeking some holy land and preordained birth
        and some ancient anarchy is loosed upon the world
        but don't distress yourself with dark imaginings
        no doubt the universe is unfolding as it should
        and the dark you see is only rain falling

        too long living not on the edge like some
        too long living in the gutter flows
        between the edges where the shadows flow
        between the edges able to see the dark
        see the dark that consumes their lives

        I'm with you in Rockland he shouts out loud
        cries from the wilderness with conviction
        is anybody out there does anybody hear him
        is Rockland just another dream in the dark
        his voice an echo of something that is no more
        a cry in the wilderness between the lines
        I'm with you in Rockland fades in the distance
        his voice disappears

Edge, page 7 of 7

       but don't get me wrong and don't get it twisted
       it may after all have been only a dream
       it may be that I have seen nothing at all
       and there was nothing at all to see in the rain
       and I have disappeared

grey is also a colour

these are not of my poetry's world:
fields of flowers waving in the wind,
wild birds singing sweet in dappled woods,
bright sunlit clouds adrift in clear cerulean skies,
ceramic women with rosy cheeks and lips;
my dark haired beauties share the shadows
as black ominous clouds sail grey skies
and crows gather in burnt out fields.

Restaurant people,
mannequin munchers posing–
Private store windows.

Sidewalk

And as they come closer
I know they are older
Than their faces will say,
Women along the way.

Studio

Framed in the window of
Unfinished buildings
Children fondling soft clay
Form heads of unknown men.

The artist smiles
As her students
Mold

I stand in the room where the painter was.
Ceiling blue with white
Down to where soft white
Hardens, and blue purples, greys to greening
Floor with bright yellow.
Grey stands a chair here and another there
Where a man can be.
The room is empty;
How can a room so empty seem so full?

Mason Jar

found, shelved filled:
a yoyo
string
gold cross
dried leaf
poem
blue ribboned
hair
one rose
letter
stained
handkerchief
life
on the mantel
jar

Transferred

Shall we call this our home,
This packing case in the country,
So hollow—
Hello! Ello lo lo lo o
—Unless we add this sound
Of children, of you, of me;
What furniture, what paint,
Can make this more a home
Than we?

Look mom. There's a big backyard!
And a tree!
Shut the door—the dog's run free!

Shall we now steal the voice
From the echo
And make this a resounding
Home?

portrait

when she's done cooking and simmering pots
paint the kitchen air with frail wisps of steam
mystical in their dreamlike soft focus
she leans forward out across the counter
her hands pressing down on the counter top
her heels raising her off the kitchen floor
as she gazes out the kitchen window
at some distant dream or nearer drama
as some rhythm in her swings her hips
softly as though anticipating me
standing erect in the doorway watching

In the prairies and mountains of the west
we knew fire well in the wild and at home,
knew its dangers and its comforts and joy,
understood the risk of getting too close.

After winter play we'd sit by the stove,
supplicants with hands outstretched to flames
that would burn us an inch or two closer,
our hearts drawn toward the fire's light and warmth.

As lovers we'd sit before the fireplace,
hovering like moths and slip ever closer
to fire hungrily lapping at the air,
to fire hungrily lapping at our hearts.

I have felt that fire in my heart for you;
I have held out my hands to feel its heat,
understood the risk of getting too close,
felt my wings drawing me into the flame.

I have seen you draw near then pull away -
say "*sometimes your love has been too intense
for me and I've shied away from the heat*" -
have spread my wings to keep you from burning.

Sit with me before the fire just for now,
let me spread my wings to hold in the warmth,
making sure the fire is only close enough
to comfort you but never burn your heart.

The Train

I have gone to the forest; you are sleeping in the town:
The fire is there in your town; I see, but I have water–
Shall I run the way, or become as the trees in the forest
Watching unquenchable you until the last spark dies,
And I take the train to town, and you ride to the forest–
Destination Eden, We come together, Love!

Now I am water wide; the land is your domain,
And I am cloud but not sky; the sky is yours alone.
Shall I rain and be yours? Or, rise to your blue bosom?
I ride your belt-line around, shuttlecock like Nancy,
Riding the train to town as your eyes come closer–
Destination Eden, We come together, Love!

City life,
Prairie Blizzard–
The wind chills.

Looking through windows:
Thunder-falls wash the lightning–
The fire is within.

dark clouds embracing
sunshine reflected above
the bright umbrella

Thunder and lightning,
Waterfall Time circles me–
Send an umbrella.

Cloudburst

Prairie city water world—
Inverse breaker waves
Cover all with drifting sea.

Alberta

there's floods in the south
the cattle have headed for the hills
the cowboys in close pursuit

the prairie reverts to primal sea
trilobites appear across the land
in this primitive place is no relief

in the streets rivers flow and deepen
distances from now to some ancient past
even canoes and drumming can't prevent

time has turned back upon itself
humans are pushed back into the hills
the woods and ancient cultures

this is not the end they say
back to the beginning of all things
born again from this shallow sea

a shadow passes across the land
something is in the air today
there's floods in the south

Inside Me

Children's story dying
                           inside me
As youth has also died
                           inside me
And now as the tears
                           inside me
Well up deep
                           inside me
There grows a doubt
                           inside me
About how there can possibly be
                           inside me
Life
                           inside me
inside me.

don't be mad at me
I ain't mad at you

don't be mad at me
I ain't mad at you

there's a lot of anger in this world
and a lot of hurt and a lot of hate

and it's there in the air
you can feel it everywhere
like the oxygen you breathe
like the rain that falls on you

there are bullies and persecutions
there's abuse and worse all around
and you see it everywhere
and you hear about it non-stop
and you feel helpless to stop

feel helpless to stop the anger
stop the hurt, stop the hate
most often just feel helpless
and lost, just lost

What can you do?
What can anyone do?

"don't be mad at me", page 2 of 6

It's them
you know it's them
the vast everyone
the normal people out there
who hate everyone who's different
who hate you
who hate me

But what can you do?
they are the many
we are the few

we are powerless
there are too many of them
the power is theirs
to change things
to just hate the other
the different
to hate us
to hurt us
to persecute and abuse us
just because

they can
and they do
they can
and they do
and what can you do?
what can I do?
what can anyone do?

don't be mad at me", page 3 of 6

        yes it's there in the air
        you can feel it everywhere
        like the oxygen you breathe
        and the anger
        the anger falls on you

        there's a lot of anger in this world
        and a lot of hurt and a lot of hate

        tag
        you're it:
        the fag
        the dyke
        the kike
        the muslim
        hell, even the Christian
        in the wrong church

        tag
        you're it:
        the dummy
        the nut case
        the crip

        you're not normal

        they hate the other
        the one
        who is different
        who acts different
        who talks different
        who's not normal

don't be mad at me", page 4 of 6

the foreigner
the spick
the wop
the jap and
the chink
the nigger
the native Indian
the white man
woman too
the uke
the kraut
the brit
the mick and
the paddy
even the yank
sometimes

everywhere
the hate, the hate, the hate
the anger seeths beneath every surface
the anger reaches out
rages
where is the focus?

tag

you say it's about you
it's them against you
the world against you
you are hurt
you are angry
you
you are angry

don't be mad at me", page 5 of 6

I ain't mad at you
don't be mad at me

I ain't mad at you
don't be mad at me

can't you see?
there is no them
except me and you
me
and you

I have met the enemy
and
he is us
she is us

I have met the enemy
deep within myself

if I have been hated
I have also hated
I have also been angry

How about you?

take a moment
stop looking for some
them
to hate
turn around and look inside
deep into yourself

don't be mad at me", page 6 of 6

       meet the enemy
       see where the enemy lives
       deep within each of us
       forgive
       just forgive
       and love
       let love and forgiveness
       replace the hate
       replace the anger
       in you

       this one choice
       this one small change
       can change your world
       may begin to change
       to change all the world

       I ain't mad at you
       don't be mad at me

       don't be mad at me
       I ain't mad at you

The words are not the same,
and yet, they are somehow
the same words we have
used so many times

Before we found our way
of using words alone
as meanings slipped
away from us, we talked

The words together meaning
what we together decided
and yet, they were somehow
not what we meant at all

To say in that brief space
and time in those few words
all there was we had
to say was not the same

Message after message passed
between us in silent codes
after the words had passed
beyond our comprehension

Of the words and meanings we
created ourselves, the words
alone and meanings separate,
we too grew apart in silence

The New Police

You start a war nobody wants or thinks is just,
then you send young men and women overseas to fight that war;
you indoctrinate them to believe everyone is the enemy
and even apparent civilians are just enemies in disguise,
then you put them in the field for five years or more
killing civilian adults and children because they may be enemies.

After a while these young men and women come home;
you give them jobs in local and state law enforcement;
you rationalize that they have the training after all,
then you give them military weapons and vehicles
just like the ones they used in war to kill civilians.

What did you think would happen?

Rainbow

Putin's troops are out in the streets
they say to subdue not to kill
to load the trucks with the bodies
kept carefully from tourist view

just dogs they say only wild dogs
though some bodies seem large for dogs
seem to cry out Russian words
cries for help muffled and cut off

trucks haul loads across the country
unload at dark and secret camps
unload at secret testing labs
unload at far and secret graves

just dogs say the soldiers wild dogs
beaten on streets and in alleys
bodies spirited off in trucks
kept carefully from the world's view

but there's a rainbow over Russia

Winter Olympics, Russia
Sochi, February, 2014

marathon

I wore my white hat against the sun
just wanted a smoke and nothing more
but the cooling spring breeze on the roof

below the streets were full of people
the heat of the day a pressure cooker
below everything was smoke and fire

I went back across the roof and down
back to work after my smoke was done
turned on the radio for the news

                        Boston Marathon Explosion
                        April 15, 2013

Circle the Wagons

on the edges of the cities,
deep in the heart of each city
in the shadows from sea to sea
hiding in plain sight in the light
in towns and reserves in the north
in the south and in all places
restless ghosts wait for the right time

we are not dead, we are not dead
the drums beat
we are not gone, we have not gone
the drums beat
out of the long silence always
hear our song
we are the people of this land
hear our hearts
hear us, hear us, hear us, hear us
our heartbeat

the dance has begun across the land
the spirits are idle no more
the people are idle no more
the ghosts are singing of justice
the people dance for their freedom
hear the drums beat across the land
the people dance for what is theirs

Circle the Wagons, page 2 of 4

        hear the hearts beat across this land
        we are not dead, we are not gone
        from the small town up to The Hill
        we sing, we dance, cry out as one
        we are the people, we are the land
        return to us what has been taken
        return to the land what has been lost

        hear the voices of the people
        risen as one from the shadows
        buried in residential schools
        in reserves, in inner city death
        we take back what has been stolen
        we will speak the old words again
        we will find our forbidden faith

        we are not dead, we are not dead
        the drums beat
        we are not gone, we have not gone
        the drums beat
        out of the long silence always
        hear our song
        we are the people of this land
        hear our hearts
        hear us, hear us, hear us, hear us
        our heartbeat

young men die on inner city streets
young women vanish in the mist
on streets and along lost highways
but before that we were taken
long before that we were hidden
hear the drums beat, we are not gone
restless ghosts we wait the right time

we are marching across this land
we are drumming across this land
we are dancing across this land
we are the spirit of this land
we are the people of this land
we have been idle far too long
we will sing out for justice now

The Queen's no longer on The Hill
treaties, agreements, and contracts
all lies, all broken, hear the drums
our chief starved to meet and be heard
our people starved but were not heard
the ghosts have waited far too long
idle no more they cry as they rise

we are marching, hear the drums beat
we are singing, our voices are loud
we are dancing, our time is now
we are the spirit of this land
we will be heard, hear the drums beat
on The Hill the man ignores us
hears the drums, says circle the wagons

we will be heard, we are not dead
the drums beat
we will be heard, we are not gone
the drums beat
the beat of our hearts as one heart
hear our hearts
we are the spirit, we are one
hear our hearts
hear us, hear us, hear us, hear us
one heartbeat

on The Hill the man ignores us
hears the drums, says circle the wagons
we are marching, hear the drums beat
we are singing, our voices are loud
we are dancing, our time is now
we are the heartbeat of this land
we will be heard, hear the drums beat

America

a lot clearer now
there's war in America.

the men are cut up
and cough from all the dust
not ready for such killing
but what can you do?

you can get used to almost anything
everybody just waits for things to change.

there are lots like that
mostly people are just tired and quiet.

you go
you just up and leave.

there's lots now that've gone
they got mad
they rioted.

here it's like that
you can feel it in the air
something could go off
you see it in the eyes.

people don't help
some do help
and America helps some
sent bacon, bread, rice, corn, flour.

February and bitter cold
four thousand cheered so loud
it shook the sky.

others said the money
would have been better spent
sending us to America
wrote and said we still support
you and the fight.

others say different
there are arguments
on the streets sometimes.

to tell truth
I just want it to end.

scene

you start out with just one thing:
a person, place, or object.

for example:

this woman in the large hat,
skirts blowing around her legs.

you look around her closely,
learn where she is standing now:

see her close by the lamp post
in the cone of light at dusk.

standing forlorn in the rain,
is she there to meet someone?

who has drawn this woman here,
could it be her secret love?

ask yourself what happens next
in the rain on the corner.

for example:

a black sedan approaches,
stops and the rear door opens.

had you noticed the music
blended with the sound of rain?

softly heard in the background,
music set the scene's blue mood.

there's a threat now, a tension
music's attack escalates.

the black sedan vanishes
along the dark rainy street.

there is only the lamplight;
there is only the soft rain.

cut and print.

Do you laugh
Picture on the wall?

You stare down
As I suffer
In my solitude.

Elsa

There is a rustle in your name, like the
passing of the years; the sound of days
falling like leaves around you, inevitably
to leave a barren scarecrow in the wind
without a rustle.

There is already a look of scarecrow in
your eyes, a certain hollow in your face
and hunger in your mien that can only grow,
like Chaos, inward upon itself.

There is a beauty about you, but it is the
derelict fantasy of a long vacant mansion
or the prairie in November rather than
that of youth in search of life.

There is a rustle that follows you as you
move, carrying autumn from room to room
and filling every room with leaves until,
one day, you shall have shed so much of
yourself that none shall be left for the
present.

Furnace burning hot
Sun hot shining on my head—
This is my summer.

The missing people mingle
In the empty room
And become real.

The insanity of an empty room creeps.

Winter
White goose–
Feathered cadaver.

White is forever,
Canada Goose bring sungreen—
Open the garden.

One by one the quiltsquares spiral
Evidence of sewing circles
Seeds of thought for winter projects.

Red sky and Rockies,
Briefly the snow turns to blood—
Death of winter day.

Scrubland bison graze,
Masters of the world they roam—
Behold now the fence.

Again turn the jar,
Snowfall in my crystal ball—
Winter day and peace.

Indian Summer

The moon shines here
Eggyolk on the river,
Orange above.
Wonder which will break first—
Eggyolk, orange,
Or will it be the day?

Dawn a Rose

And I was One who rose
To meet Another there
Who lightly rose as Dawn
Across my mind's East Sky;

Like light I rose to walk
The garden rows of clouds
Alight with flaring roses,
Rose rendezvous for two;

Rose to walk a shining
Garden full of roses
In regimental rows
to honour Dawn a rose -

As you: the Sun arose.

The news of the world
slips past at sunset:

days pass like pages.

Previous Publications

Some poems included in *Agapé: Heaven & Earth* have previously been published in the following.

Periodicals: Ball State University Forum, Bardic Echoes, Canadian Golden West, The Creative Review, The Creative Urge, The Dalhousie Review, Fellowship in Prayer, Generation '81, Gnosis, Green's Magazine, Janus & SCTH, The Lunatic Fringe, Origins II, The Other Side, Other Voices, Poetry E Train (online magazine), Quintessence, Salt #9, The Sarnia Entertainer, Special Song, Stimulus, The Tower (Tower Poetry Society, McMaster University), This Singing World (The Hartford Courant), Verse Afire (The Ontario Poetry Society), and Wax Poetry and Art Magazine.

Anthologies: That Not Forgotten (Hidden Brook Press, 2012), Pine's the Canadian Tree (Tower Poetry Society, McMaster University, 1974), The Tower Exhibition (catalogue & anthology, Sarnia Public Art Gallery, 1973), and Alberta Poetry Yearbook (Canadian Authors' Association, 1970, 1971, 1972).

Books: Spirit Quest (Dark Matter Press, 2014), On Edge (Dark Matter Press, 2012), Audio-Visuals (catalogue and poetry chapbook, Sarnia Public Art Gallery, 1972), and Reflection (R. D. MacKenzie, 1966).

Recordings (with Poem de Terre): War & Love (2006), Live at Newlands Pavilion, Parts 1 & 2 (2004), Assume Nothing (1999), Pyramid (1995), and Windfall (1994)

Television: Creative Minds hosted by Lini Grol (St. Catharines, Ontario)

Radio: Finding a Voice hosted by Bruce Kauffman (CFRC, Kingston, Ontario), Howl hosted by Nik Beat (CIUT, Toronto, Ontario)

Paintings, wood-cut art prints, and sculptures: by Herbert Ariss, Margot Ariss, G. Brender à Brandis, James Evans, Lini Grol, Mercedes Horne, R. D. MacKenzie, Marlis Saunders, and Stania Slahor.

About Bob MacKenzie

Bob MacKenzie's poetry has appeared in hundreds of publications across North America and as far away as Australia and India, including Salt, The Dalhousie Review, The University of Windsor Review, The Tower, Ball State University Forum and many more.

Bob has published fourteen books of poetry and prose-fiction and his work has been featured in numerous anthologies. His poems have been reproduced by visual artists and sculptors and a public art gallery has devoted an entire visual arts exhibition to his poetry. He is possibly the only poet to have versions of his poetry owned by the Canada Council's National Art Bank.

Bob has received a number of awards for his writing, including "On Edge" winner of the poetry category in the international Sharp Writ Book Awards for 2012 and of a bronze medal in the 2013 international Readers Favorite Book Awards, novels "Ghost Shadow: Unfinished Sins" and "Another Eternity" winners in their respective categories of bronze medals in the 2012 international Readers Favorite Book Awards, and an Ontario Arts Council grant for literature.

On his own throughout his career and for eighteen years with the performance ensemble Poem de Terre, Bob has performed much of his poetry live with original music and has released seven albums with Poem de Terre. Throughout his career, Bob has also presented performances by other artists, beginning in the summer of 1966 with two major readings at the Allied Arts Centre in Calgary that featured a young George Bowering, later to be Poet Laureate of Canada, along with other Calgary poets, musicians, visual artists, and sculptors.

Photo Credits:
front and back cover Rocky Mountain scenes by Shirley Jean Young
front cover author portrait by Adelita
back cover author portrait by Beverly Jilson
author biography portrait, Kate Morgan

www.ingramcontent.com/pod-product-compliance
Lightning Source LLC
Chambersburg PA
CBHW071421160426
43195CB00013B/1765